Pebble®
Plus

LET'S LOOK AT COUNTRIES

LET'S LOOK AT

SYRIA

BY NIKKI BRUNO CLAPPER

CAPSTONE PRESS
a capstone imprint

Pebble Plus is published by Capstone Press,
1710 Roe Crest Drive, North Mankato, Minnesota 56003
www.mycapstone.com

Library of Congress Cataloging-in-Publication Data
Names: Clapper, Nikki Bruno, author.
Title: Let's look at Syria / by Nikki Bruno Clapper.
Description: North Mankato, Minnesota : Capstone Press, [2018] | Series:
   Pebble plus. Let's look at countries | Includes bibliographical references
   and index. | Audience: Ages 4-8.
Identifiers: LCCN 2017037881 (print) | LCCN 2017038380 (ebook) | ISBN
   9781515799313 (eBook PDF) | ISBN 9781515799191 (hardcover) | ISBN
   9781515799252 (pbk.)
Subjects: LCSH: Syria--Juvenile literature.
Classification: LCC DS93 (ebook) | LCC DS93 .C54 2018 (print) | DDC
   956.91--dc23
LC record available at https://lccn.loc.gov/2017037881

Editorial Credits
Juliette Peters, designer; Tracy Cummins, media researcher; Laura Manthe, production specialist

Photo Credits
Getty Images: AFP PHOTO/MICHALIS KARAGIANNIS, 14, Diaa Al Din/Anadolu Agency, 17, Ibrahim Ebu Leysi/Anadolu Agency, 12; iStockphoto: jcarillet, 13, urf, 15; Shutterstock: Anton_Ivanov, 6-7, Cover Top, IKostiuchok, 21, Jakob Fischer, Cover Middle, Cover Back, Kanunnikov Pavel, 22 Top, Leif Stenberg, 1, Martchan, Cover Bottom, 3, Megerya Anna, 9, nale, 4, OBJM, 5, 22-23, 24, Strannik_fox, 10, Tanya Stolyarevskaya, 19, Yerbolat Shadrakhov, 11

Note to Parents and Teachers

The Let's Look at Countries set supports national curriculum standards for social studies related to people, places, and culture. This book describes and illustrates Syria. The images support early readers in understanding the text. The repetition of words and phrases helps early readers learn new words. This book also introduces early readers to subject-specific vocabulary words, which are defined in the Glossary section. Early readers may need assistance to read some words and to use the Table of Contents, Glossary, Read More, Internet Sites, Critical Thinking Questions, and Index sections of the book.

Printed in the United States of America.
010774S18

TABLE OF CONTENTS

Where Is Syria?

Syria is a country in Asia.

It is part of the Middle East.

Syria is about the size of the

U.S. state of North Dakota.

Its capital is Damascus.

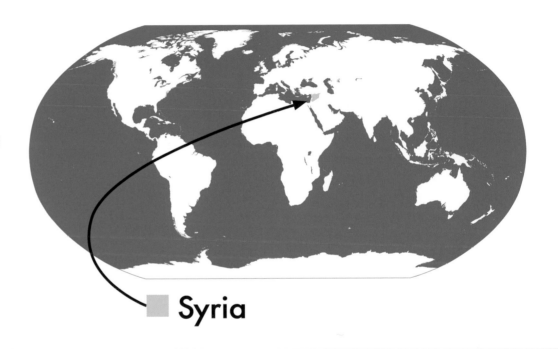

■ Syria

A Rocky Land

Much of Syria is a
desert of rock and gravel.

Dust storms cloud the air.

Mountain ranges rise
in the west.

Two bodies of water

are important to Syria.

The Mediterranean Sea is on

the west coast. The Euphrates

River flows in the northeast.

In the Wild

Animals roam Syria's desert. Lizards and vipers hide in the rocks. The jerboa jumps around at night. It is a small rodent with long back legs.

lizard

jerboa

People

Most people in Syria are Arabs. Other groups are Kurds and Armenians. Most Syrians live in the western half of the country.

On the Job

Some Syrians farm wheat or cotton for a living. Others help people. They may work in hospitals, schools, or restaurants.

A Holy Month

Ramadan is a major holiday in Syria. It is a holy month in the Islam religion. People do not eat in the daytime. They feast at night.

Ramadan feast

At the Table

Syrians eat a lot of meat, flatbread, and salads. One popular meal is kibbeh. Kibbeh are wheat balls filled with lamb or beef.

kibbeh

Famous Site

Broken stone columns rise from the desert. This is the ancient city of Palmyra. It was once a place of great wealth. Today it is in ruins.

21

QUICK SYRIA FACTS

Syrian flag

Name: Syrian Arab Republic
Capital: Damascus
Other major cities: Aleppo, Homs, Hama
Population: 17,185,170 (July 2016 estimate)
Size: 71,498 square miles (185,180 sq km)
Languages: Arabic, Kurdish, Armenian
Money: Syrian pound

GLOSSARY

capital—the city in a country where the government is based

column—a pillar that supports a building

gravel—a mixture of sand, pebbles, and broken rocks

Islam—a religion founded in the 600s by Muhammad

jerboa—a nocturnal jumping rodent of Asia and Africa

ruins—the remains of a building or other things that have fallen down or been destroyed

viper—a snake that kills its prey with poison called venom

wealth—state of having lots of money

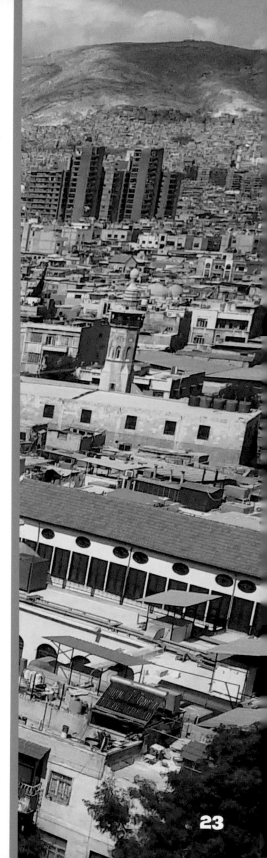

READ MORE

Arnold, Caroline. *A Day and Night in the Desert.* Caroline Arnold's Habitats. North Mankato, Minn.: Picture Window Books, 2015.

Bullard, Lisa. *Rashad's Ramadan and Eid al-Fitr.* Holidays and Special Days. Minneapolis: Millbrook Press, 2012.

Murray, Julie. *Syria.* Explore the Countries. Minneapolis: Abdo Pub., 2017.

INTERNET SITES

Use FactHound to find Internet sites related to this book.

Visit *www.facthound.com*

Just type 9781515799191 and go.

 Check out projects, games and lots more at
www.capstonekids.com

CRITICAL THINKING QUESTIONS

1. Look at the photo on page 11. How do you think a jerboa's long ears might help it live in the desert?

2. What is a column? What do the columns of Palmyra look like?

3. What are two foods that Syrians eat often?

INDEX